**Tales for the Weird, Pessimistic and altogether Unus
A Collection of short stories
by Ethan Obi-Wan Couldrey**

Table of Contents

For Obi
"I remember you, so you are Eternal"
Love Dad

To the Exact Detail

I came across this story shortly before we entered Covid-19 lockdown. And am only just now getting around to putting it to print. Before we go any further, some introductions are in order. It is not important for the context of this story for you to know my name, though it is important for you to know some things about me.

Firstly, and most importantly, I am a fan and collector of ghost stories. I started by reading fiction, the likes of Charles Dickens and M.R James' excellent works lined my shelves and indeed my audiobook library for some time. This, in turn, evolved into a fascination of finding a real ghost story.

Not just your regular camera footage of a table moving itself or a blurry face or hard to make out staticky voice, the likes of which you might see on Most Haunted. But a truly, Gothic ghost story. The kind of which you find in those Victorian and Edwardian stories.

A second, less important but equally relevant fact about myself, is that I am an enthusiast of steam engines. Growing up with the likes of Thomas and Friends and indeed having a grandfather who used to let me play with his model railway, has left me with a deep fondness for steam trains and model railways that over the years has never seemed to leave me.

So now that you have all the relevant information. On with the story.

It must have been late November in 2019 when a friend of mine approached me with a local newspaper from a small village near Brighton named Lower Overleigh. My friend travels often and must have passed through the village and knowing my interests, picked up the paper to show me.

There on the front page of the week's issue of the Lower Overleigh Witness was the headline "My Model Railway is Haunted!" I must say, seeing the headline with the accompanying picture of a rather stereotypically "nerdy" train enthusiast standing in front of his model layout, amused me more than it did intrigue me. But it was only after I read the full article, that my amusement died down and my intrigue began to grow.

The article itself really wasn't much to write home about. Your typical tabloid supernatural tale with a model railway twist. "The points changed by themselves, and my locomotives kept moving," the sort of stuff that you would expect, but there was something about the subject of the article and this rather nerdy man that intrigued me. He was a middle-aged man I would have said late 40's maybe early 50's, he wore a checked shirt and rather large glasses. He sported a comb over and was quite pale. The very image of what people think model enthusiasts look like, but there was something about his face. The expression he wore in the accompanying photograph, to me at least, conveyed true fear, like he was truly scared of this supposed apparition! His interview in the article too, seemed odd, very vague and brief descriptions, as if he was being distant, as if he was holding some dark terrible truth away from us all.

This oddity sparked my interest, and I ended up tracking down the subject of the article, one Christopher West and contacted him. I explained my interest in both the supernatural, steam power and how I read the article and would like to meet with him to get a more first-hand account of the events. To my surprise, he responded quickly accepting my invitation, asking me to meet with him the following Tuesday.

So just like that, I was on my way to Lower Overleigh. I won't bore you with the details of my journey, but I did take the train. The Village itself was much as my friend described it, nothing to write home about. The most interesting part of the village seemed to be the railway. Well, that and a rather melancholy statue of a woman in Victorian dress by the rail side.

I eventually met with Chris at his home, and he greeted me nicely enough. We had some tea and he escorted me to his basement where his model layout, (seemingly an exact recreation of how Lower Overleigh might have been in the 1880's) resided. For a while I was treated to a very long speech from Chris about his layout, the research he had done to get it as exact to his home village as possible, the different locomotives and so on. As he droned on, my attention drew to his face, to that same dread-laden expression I had seen in the newspaper article.

I eventually convinced him to tell me more about the supernatural goings on in this basement, his expression worsened, but he nodded and explained that to understand what happened on his layout, I must first know a local legend.

In the late 1880's, it is believed that a woman threw herself in front of a train on a cold winter's night. No one knows why, but the moment has been mythised in the village, the lady being dubbed the Overleigh Maiden. The statue that I had seen by the rail side was erected in the unknown woman's memory.

He explained that it had all started when he had come down and saw that his layout was covered in fake snow and ice, depicting the railway in winter. I looked around seeing the layout as he had just described and asked what was wrong with that. He replied that when he had gone to bed the previous night, his layout depicted the railway in summer.

I sat in somewhat stunned silence for a moment, before asking Chris to go on. He stated that he thought the change in season was odd but assumed that one of his modelling friends had done it as a joke, but after asking them they had all denied tampering with his layout. Still, he assumed he was victim to nothing more than a bizarre practical joke and had gone about his daily routine. The next day however, Chris told me, was when things got truly bizarre.

He explained that the next day he had come downstairs to find that by model recreation of the Overleigh Maiden's bridge there now stood a small plastic model woman, standing in the center of the bridge. I immediately cut in asking if the model resembled the statue of the Overleigh Maiden. Chris could only offer a grave nod in response. I apologised for interrupting and asked him to please continue.

Chris told me that he tried to remove the figurine to inspect it, but no matter how hard he pulled it. It would not budge. He instead decided to note down his findings. As crazy as they seemed, so that he could keep track of the bizarre changes. Over the next days, Chris recorded that the figurine, slowly but surely moved closer and closer to the edge of the bridge, only a couple of milometers a day until, eventually. I cut in again, 'She jumped?' Chris shook his head again 'she was pushed'. I looked confused before, again apologising for interrupting and asking him to explain.

He explained that a few days into the figurine moving she had been joined by a figurine of a man. From what Chris could make out on the small figure the man was average height and build, brown hair, possibly with a beard and wearing a suit with a large top hat and a scarf around his neck. They seemed to chat for a while over the days, before things started to become violent. Chris described the agony of this struggle between these two people, playing out over days like some kind of macabre dance.

Eventually the struggle came to ahead with the man pinning the maiden to the handrail of the bridge, but he pushed her too hard. Instead of being pinned, she instead went over the rail, falling over days and days. Everyday suspended lower in mid-air, until eventually gravity took it's hold, and she fell right in front of one of his model trains, the model that perfectly recreated the train that hit the Overleigh Maiden.

I sat for a few moments, words failing me for the time being before Chris asked me "You know what this means?" Still being in a slight state of shock I absently shook my head, still trying to process what I had just heard.

"It means." He continued "That she didn't throw herself in front of the train she was pushed! That's why she contacted me! So, I knew! So, I could tell people!" I looked up to him finally finding me words as he veered off into his ramblings. I asked how could he know that? And even if it were true why would she tell us now? Why would she wait over 140 years to tell us that the legend around her death was false? What could we do? Her murderer was as long dead as she was and would be damn near impossible to find.

Chris looked to the floor for a moment seeming to take in what I said. A few times I thought of asking if he was okay but decided against it. Eventually he got up and moved over to his layout and grabbed something, bringing it over to show me. It was a model figure of a Victorian man. It was surprisingly well detailed figure. I could make out his short beard, light complexion, even at this scale. The bright blue cravat and top hat he sported further helped to distinguish him from the other rather dull covered Victorian men I could see recreated on his layout.

I looked at Chris for a moment, he stared back expectantly. "What's this?" I asked, trying to remain as polite as I could. "That's your answer." Chris exclaimed, his rambling tone back in full force. "This is the model of the man who murdered her! I didn't make it! The model of the maiden disappeared when the train hit but this one stayed. It's a lead! Our biggest lead to find out who killed her!"

Chris then offered me the model. I did hesitate for a moment but decided to take it.

Yes, even with this figurine as a lead, my chances of finding information about someone who died over a century ago were slim at best, even if they were a well-known businessman in their day, but I must admit that like Chris, my interest was piqued. "Alright." I said beginning to stand "Is there somewhere in the village that holds public records I could look through?" Chris nodded explaining that the small local library had a small record room that may have a list of names and photographs from the period.

I agreed to stay on for a few more days and check out the library to see what I could find. We had another cup of tea, and I asked Chris if he's help me search for a lead, but he insisted that he stay at home with his layout, "Just in case the Maiden sends us another clue". So, after finishing another tense cup of tea I finally left Chris' house and checked myself in to a local Bed and Breakfast. That night I had time to think about my encounter. Chris was odd sure, but he didn't seem to be lying. Was he genuine? Or had he convinced himself of what he saw? I looked at the model figure one last time before falling asleep. Hoping that I would get my answer tomorrow.

The next morning, I decided to get an early start on research. I had a light breakfast then headed straight to the library. For a small village, Lower Overleigh's library was quite sizeable. Nothing when compared to city libraries, but still sizeable. The building itself was Victorian in design. A plaque confirmed that it was built in 1885. The library was called the Edwin Lane public library.

I entered and was met with the undeniably nostalgic aroma of old books and stone; you could practically smell the history of the place. After explaining my interest in the Village's records to the kind old Librarian, I was escorted to the records room.

It was a mass of records stacked nearly as high as the ceiling of the cramped back room. All around me were records and loose scraps of paper stacked in some sort of chaotic order. In the center of the room was a computer that seemed to be from the late 90's or early 2000's, boxy and white, with a large keyboard and oversized mouse.

I sat down and began to use the old computers archaic filing system searching for any influential figures in the villages history that matched Chris' mystery miniature. I must admit, my hopes were low, even if the events that Chris described were true and the Overleigh Maiden was trying to oust her killer. It was unlikely that I would be able to find him. Unless of course, he was someone of relevance to the village, someone influential to its history. It turned out, he was.

After searching for a few hours for vague things like, "1880's important locals" and "Lower Overleigh important Victorians" I came across an old photograph. One of someone who matched the model to a tee. Young, big top hat, everything about him was correct, even the date of the photograph was the late 1880's.

He was a perfect match to the mysterious model! So, I looked up who he was, and the answer shook me somewhat. His name was Edwin Lane, he was the person that this library was named after. It turned out that Lane was an instrumental part of Industrial Revolution in Lower Overleigh. The small village had stayed relatively unchanged by the events around it until Lane came along and brought industry, steam power, factories, new buildings and even the railway to his home. Looking through the records it seems he was regarded as a hero in the local history.

A pioneer of progress.

So, then, why did he kill the Overleigh Maiden? Well, after a few more hours of research, I found the answer to that question as well. There was a long-standing rumour that Lane had a mistress. If the rumours were proven, it would have been very damaging for Mr. Lane. His wife was the daughter of an important railway businessman who allowed Lane to oversee the Overleigh line. If he was found to be unfaithful, he would have lost everything.

It all suddenly clicked into place, the Overleigh Maiden was Lanes Mistress. He must have invited her to rendezvous and the bridge and then seized his opportunity to silence her, all for the sake of his career. I sat reading more and more about Lane, everything checked out, I turned away from the computer for a moment, gathering my thoughts. The task I had though impossible, finding the Overleigh Maidens killer, had just been achieved, but the question remained, what now? I decided to go back to Chris and share my findings with him. What we did next, we would decide together.

I left the library and started to make may way towards Chris' house, jogging slightly with the excitement of my discovery. As I arrived at Chris' house however, my excitement was soon replaced by confusion.

There were police cars outside his house, men in overalls under police escort were taking out his furniture and loading it into moving vans also parked outside of his house. I approached them and asked them what they were doing. They explained that Chris West had been reported missing a few weeks ago, just after he was in the local newspaper, the missing persons case had been filed after none of the neighbours had seen him for two weeks and the house had been locked up.

They were only now just getting around to clearing out the house.

For a moment I thought it to be a poorly timed practical joke on Chris' part. How could he be missing? I'd just seen him yesterday. I tried to explain that to the officer, but he insisted it was impossible for me to have been inside the house. I suggested that maybe Chris had reappeared and let me in, but they said apart from my testament no one else had seen or heard from him. I gave a statement to the police, leaving out the haunting details, thinking it unwise to share, they thanked me for the information and asked me to let them know if Chris ever tried to make contact.

I watched the clean out of Chris' house, with the small crowd that had gathered. trying to wrap my head around everything that had happened in the last few days. Everything swirled, nothing added up. I decided to stop thinking and just watched this person (who I apparently had been the first and last to see in weeks) possessions get cleared out.

Finally, they started to bring out Chris' model railway. I pushed past the crowd to get a better look. Which is when I saw it. An image that I still have dreams about. An image that has put me off writing this story for so long, there on the bridge of Chris' Overleigh model were two figurines, posed in conversation.

One model was that of the Overleigh Maiden, the second model, a new model I had not seen before was a figure of a middle-aged man, rather nerdy and wearing thick glasses. A model with the exact likeness of Chris.

The Unknown Soldier

My second story, I came across following a tip given by a friend of mine who worked at a local care-home, she knew my interest in ghost stories and thought this was something I would enjoy. She told me that a resident had told her a story, that had in her own words "chilled her to the bone". I visited this care home and what follows is a direct transcript of an audio interview I conducted with the resident Mr. Alfred Noakes.

Tape Start

"Good afternoon, Alfie, can you tell me your war ghost story please…….

Fine, I suppose I should start with a bit of background.

My Names Alfred but everyone calls me Alfie, always thought Alfred was a bit too much of a posh name for me so I've always preferred Alfie, sounds less like a schoolmaster. Anyway, I am one of the last surviving veterans of World War One and I've recently been asked to rely on my experience of war for the 90th Anniversary of the war starting by my local newspaper.

I signed up when I was 16 in 1915, hard to think I was ever that young now, after I've had my letter from the queen four, no five times over now…

Sorry I keep getting distracted,

I'll carry on with the story, I signed up too young. It sounded so patriotic when I signed up, fighting the Fritzies back and doing my duty for King and Country, plus all my friends were signing up so of course I did. I was a foolish child, and the reality of the situation hit me hard. As soon as I got in one of those Western Front Trenches. The death, destruction, bullets and bombs flying at you in every direction, it knocked any fantasy of what warfare would be from my mind and forced me to accept the gritty reality, tends to happen when you see good friends die or succumb to shellshock, that knocks any preconceived notion of how honourable war is right out of you. It was hell plain and simple, absolute hell.

Right so the story you want me to tell, if, you're sure?"

"Oh yes Alfie I'm sure, indeed I'm fascinated"

"Well, it must've been around 1917, you never get used to the horrors of war, but I'd gotten familiar with it enough to be numb to it, used to its horrors and losses. I woke up in my tiny bunk and went to work, grabbing my rifle and eating the moldy biscuits and drinking the tea whose leaves had been used countless times. I called that my breakfast.

I then peered precariously over the edge of the trench, hoping once again that a stray bullet wouldn't immediately hit me in the face. The gunfire and shelling from both sides started early and ended late, you got used to it or you went mad listening to it. Luckily today was not my day to die.

I continued my patrol, trying to keep warm in this blistering cold, blowing into my likely frostbitten hands as I continued to look over the ridge, staring at the vast vacuous expanse of no man's land. With its barren frosty fields and odd clusters of barbed wire, it was hard for me to think that there was another trench on the other side, it felt like we were fighting an invisible enemy. Suppose that made it easier for both sides, spending most of our time shelling and firing at people we couldn't properly see. Save for those chaotic hellish times when we went over the trench, when you could actually look into your enemies' eyes and see, just another scared boy doing his duty to his country.

I much preferred trench combat, less thinking more shooting.

Anyway, as I looked over the ridge, I noticed something. A spec in the sky, just a black dot soaring over no man's land. At first, I assumed it was a bird, but it was travelling too fast and getting bigger. It wasn't until it was on top of us 'til I realised what it was. A gas bomb! I sounded the alarm and shouted till my lungs hurt, but it was no use. Before I knew it gas was flooding the trench. I tried to do what I was told, taking a, I hope you don't mind me using this language, piss on my hanky and covering my face.

It's what we'd been taught and apparently it did work, some science I didn't get but I didn't care to, I just didn't want Mustard Gas in my lungs, I'd seen what it had done to my mates. But I couldn't go, not enough drinking or maybe I was just nervous, but I couldn't go. I tried to run but no matter how hard I tried I couldn't find a way out that wasn't already blocked off. I started to think, is this it? Is this how I die? I was just 18 and I was thinking about my own death. What would it feel like? I was brought up a Christian but when you're staring death in the face you start to doubt it all. Would I go to heaven? Would it hurt? My short life was just finished flashing before my eyes and I think I had finally accepted my fate when through the thick misty death an arm shot out and grabbed me, pulling me clear of the vapours embrace.

He pulled me through the gas, as fast as lightning. I held my breath as best I could, but it didn't seem to faze him. I could only make out his back, like me he was wearing the green uniform of a soldier, I assumed he must have a gas mask on. Eventually we came out of the gases deadly embrace, to the freedom of the other side of the trench. I thanked him for his help and asked his name. He said no problem and- wait, now that I think about it, I recognised that voice, it was a voice I'd heard before. Frank's voice. My best mate, one of the lads I signed up with, but it couldn't have been him, he got killed back in 1916, bullet straight to the skull, quick, I remember taking solace in that.

So, this soldier had the voice of my best friend. He continued, "My names ----" As he spoke his name all I heard was static, you know like from the wireless when it's not tuned in, it was an extremely loud static that made me cover my ears and close my eyes.

Thinking back, I should've left them closed.

Then he finally turned around to face me and I nearly screamed. Where his face was supposed to be there was nothing. A white void on a blank canvas. Indentations where a mouth, nose and eyes were supposed to be covered by skin, as if a skin mask had been stretched over a normal person's face. Even his ears were merely indented shapes, hinting at something human under that layer of stretched pale skin.

He spoke again, this time with a different but all too recognisable voice, my father's voice.

It had been so long since I'd heard it that I didn't even recognise it at first. My dad had been drafted in 1914 when the war had broken out and was KIA soon after. That familiar soothing growl, that voice that always made me feel like everything was going to be okay, was now so sinister, so unnatural, so wrong, as it came from this mockery of a human being.

The voice said to me that we needed to keep moving and to "snap out of it my boy!"

I stared dumbfounded. Snap out of it? The faceless soldier that spoke in other people's voices was telling me to snap out of it. Though there wasn't much time to question that. I heard enemy fire and movement from behind us and even though it terrified me, when the faceless soldier offered me his hand, I took it. Still not sure why, guess I knew it wasn't going to hurt me and I reckoned it was better going with this thing and having a chance to live, than staying here and getting caught or shot by the German forces.

We continued to run across the expanse of nothingness behind the trench. Every now and then, the faceless man kept checking on me, speaking in a different voice of someone I loved each time. My father, my mother, my best friend, my first love. Each time it made me wince. Each time it made me scared.

We continued to walk together through the night before we got close to the eastern trench. "Well, here we are." said the faceless man, speaking with Frank's voice once again. I looked back to him nodding softly, feeling completely numb and cold towards everything.

We made our way towards the trench, the faceless man leading me toward the allies. When we got close a group of British soldiers peered over the trench, shouting at us to stop and pointing their rifles at us. I hadn't thought this through. They were going to be terrified of the Soldier, same as I was.

But they weren't desperate, they weren't alone.

They were a unified front, and they would gun us down out of fear, I would die beside a monster and my story would be lost to time.

But they didn't fire. Instead, they greeted us with open arms. It was as if nothing was wrong. As if they couldn't tell that I was terrified or that the bloke next to me didn't have a bloody face!

They just said Well done for getting back safe and sound.

Had I gone mad?

Or had everyone else?

It was hard to tell that at the best of times in those trenches, but this was ridiculous. I was taken by the friendly soldiers to a first aid tent for inspection, and I never saw the faceless soldier again.

Well, that's my story. I know it's not too long and the ending is a bit of an anti-climax. I just continued to fight the war until it was over, made new friends watched them die, can't tell you how happy I was when 1919, no, wait sorry 1918 came around and the war finished.

I still wish I knew what the hell that faceless soldier was and why it's only now that I'm remembering how weird it was. It's as if I'd forgotten and all the memories came back and for the 90th anniversary of it all.

Sorry, why am I recording this again?"

"Thank you, Alfie, thank you very much indeed"

Tape End

Whilst I enjoyed Alfie's story, and it did pique my interest I thought nothing more of it and filed the tape in my archive for later transcription and maybe use, that was until my friend told me a few weeks later that Mr. Noakes had passed away in his sleep and she handed me a copy of the patients notes that's she had photocopied for me, below is a direct copy of these notes.

Patient Records Extract dated two weeks prior to me meeting Alfie

Patient notes for Alfred Noakes aged 105, conducted by Dr. Sipher.

Patient is still very able for their age. It really is impressive how mentally competent they have been able to remain after over a century of life.

However, it seems like that competence is to come to an end. The patient is now showing signs of early onset Alzheimer's Disease. They are muddling dates and details in their memories and most Importantly they have fabricated a story to help account for these misremembrance's.

The patient is recounting a seemingly real event from 1917 when the trench that they were serving in was hit with mustard gas and they were pulled free from the fumes by a fellow soldier.

The patient recounts that this other soldier had no face and spoke with the voices of people he once knew.

I believe that this is his minds attempt to make up for the guilt he must feel of forgetting the man who saved his life.

He can no longer picture his face, so his memory gives them none.

He doesn't remember his name, so the soldier doesn't give one.

He can't remember his voice, so the soldier speaks in the voices of other people he can remember.

I have never seen the mind do this, but it does make sense. Extreme guilt (in war survivors) can cause people to block off or change their memories to ignore that guilt and yes trauma.

(possible PTSD Will need to consult local MH services)

The patient may have already been repressing these traumatic memories but his Alzheimer's deteriorating his memories, coupled with the guilt of forgetting someone who saved his life has caused him to concoct this fantastical story of a monstrous faceless man.

The patient does seem more cognitive and aware than others of his age with Alzheimer's however, which still puzzles me, but his story cannot possibly be true, can it?

No, it can't which is why I am recommending we continue to monitor the patients progress and note down any other deteriorations.

End notes.

SCP-7977

My third and final story my friends is one that I find challenging at best, throughout my travels I have on several occasions been given proposed reports from a secretive organisation known as the SCP Foundation. This foundation allegedly

"*is entrusted by governments around the world to capture and contain various unexplained paranormal phenomena that defy the known laws of nature (referred to as "anomalies", "SCP objects", "SCPs", or informally as "skips"). They include living beings and creatures, artifacts and objects, locations and places, abstract concepts, and incomprehensible entities which display supernatural abilities or other extremely unusual properties. If left uncontained, many of the more dangerous anomalies will pose a serious threat to humans or even all life on Earth. All information regarding the existence of the Foundation and SCPs are strictly withheld from the general public in order to prevent mass hysteria that would supposedly occur if they were leaked, and allow human civilization to continue functioning under a masquerade of "normalcy"*

"Special Containment Procedures" of a given SCP object. In a typical scenario, an SCP object is assigned a unique identification number"

Reference Wikipedia (link: https://en.wikipedia.org/wiki/SCP_Foundation#cite_note-SCiP-8)

Most of the time I discard these reports as fanfiction, a product of a of a mass internet writing project, BUT one, yes just one has given me a degree of reasonable doubt to question my dismissal of all of these reports.

This report was given to me recently following a spate of deaths in my local community, my source (redacted) was genuinely fearful of the repercussions of exposing this report's contents or even its existence, but they also knew given my background I may uncover the truth myself.

Below is the report I was handed, its either great fan fiction or we all may have been lied to our entire lives by our own governments.

It is worth noting that my source seems to have disappeared and is no longer returning any of my contact attempts with them.

SCP-7977 Case Report

Item #: SCP-7977

Object Class: Safe

Special Containment Procedures: SCP-7977 is to be kept in a standard class 1 containment locker Within Storage Wing-24 in Site-23.

Personnel of Level 4 or higher security clearance are permitted to run tests on SCP-7977 after filling out the appropriate paperwork. D-Class personnel used in tests of SCP-7977 should not be exposed to SCP-7977 for more than forty-eight (48) hours to prevent the risk of prolonged addiction or ███████████████. Any D-Class personnel affected by the anomalous effects of SCP-7977 are to be referred to Site Therapists to receive addiction treatment.

Please contact Dr. Churchward if access of SCP-7977 is expected to exceed seventy-two (72) hours.

Description:

SCP-7977 is a standard metal drinking straw measuring 8cm tall. The metal appears to be stainless steel and all tests conducted on SCP-7977 to determine the material it is made from appear to confirm this (despite the numerous anomalous effects of SCP-7977 that would suggest otherwise).

The anomalous effects of SCP-7977 become apparent when it is placed in any container filled with any amount of liquid.

Any human that drinks from the straw reports tasting their favourite beverage despite what the actual liquid may be. Reported beverages include Tea, Coffee, Diet Cola, Lemonade and ███████████. SCP-7977 also seems to negate any harmful effects that a human would suffer from consuming dangerous liquids when they are drunk through SCP-7977.

Liquids tested include, liquid nitrogen, hydrochloric acid, chloride dioxide and carbaryl pesticide. All test subjects that drank these liquids using SCP-7977 suffered no ill consequences and some even requested a second helping.

A side effect of SCP-7977's anomalous transformative effects is that liquid transformed no longer has any hydrational value and in fact dehydrates the subject using SCP-7977.

In tandem any subject using SCP-7977 to drink will begin to exhibit signs of addiction to only using SCP-7977 to drink. Becoming hysterical if SCP-7977 is taken off of them and exhibiting symptoms of withdrawal. If left alone, subjects using SCP-7977 will continue to only drink liquids through SCP-7977 until they eventually expire due to extreme dehydration or [REDACTED].

Subjects afflicted with severe addiction to SCP-7977 can be treated by being removed from the vicinity of SCP-7977 and undergoing no fewer than Twelve (12) months of vigorous addiction therapy similar to that used to treat crippling drug addiction or chronic alcoholics.

SCP-7977 was discovered in 20██ in ████████ England after a coroner's report noted the strange death of a Mr ██████ who exhibited all the signs of dehydration yet had a stomach full of liquid.

Agents were dispatched and after interviewing both the coroner and the police who had discovered the body of Mr ███████ and Mr ██████'s family, discovered SCP-7977.

After determining the anomalous qualities of SCP-7977, it was confiscated by the Foundation. Class B amnestics were administered to the affected officers and civilians, wiping their memories.

Report End

Over the Edge (a short story)

What was she doing here? Standing on this old creaking bridge, she peered over the side and noted the height of the water. It was higher than she had ever seen. A flood must be due soon.

Why was she here? What was she doing on a cold May night in the year of our lord 1886, standing her arms over a barrier and a sleeping infant within those arms? Of course, the question was a rhetorical one. She knew what she was doing. Any passer-by could see what she was doing, contemplating throwing the child.

She had had the infant (who she had taken to calling Alex) out of wedlock, and his father had fled before they could be married. Raising the child alone would be dangerous. She could be thrown from her home, and no one would help her.

They would think her a whore and go out of their way to avoid her.

She looked over the edge again. The harshness of the water further deepening the conflict within her. This must be the best option. To end the child's life. Wasn't it? This had seemed so easy in her mind. Toss the child off the bridge, it dies painlessly, and she could go on with her noble life, and the child would never grow up being persecuted for something he couldn't control, but now she stood there, and it seemed impossible.

Looking into his soft, round sapphire eyes, she found that she could not loosen her grip on the bundle of blankets the child was wrapped in. In fact, her grip seemed to tighten. Why is this so hard? She contemplated, beginning to get hysterical with it all. She screamed as if to scare herself into letting go of the child.

The scream roused the child from his sleep, and he began to cry, calling out wordlessly to his mother.

She began to become misty-eyed. She continued to hold the child there, the current of the river below surging and splashing upwards, as if the water itself was beckoning her. She tried to pull the child from her grip into a far colder embrace.

She looked at the bawling infant a final time.

The conflict within her seemed to reach its natural conclusion.

With one solid motion, she pulled the child from the edge and into her tender embrace.

The two stood there for a while longer, crying silently with each other.

What had she done?

No, she pushed these thoughts from her mind.

Life will be tough, but her son deserves a chance at life.

Alex deserves a chance.

She continued to weep with her son as they made their way solemnly off the bridge and into a hard but hopeful future.

Printed in Great Britain
by Amazon